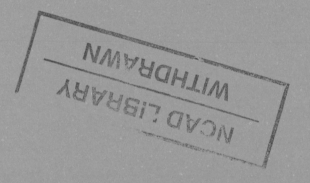

DOGS AND CHAIRS
Designer Pairs

Cristina Amodeo

With 49 illustrations

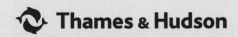
Thames & Hudson

―――――――――

'Eventually everything connects –
people, ideas, objects...
the quality of the connections
is the key to quality per se.'

Charles Eames

―――――――――

IT ALL BEGAN THE DAY
I ACCIDENTALLY SAT ON A DOG.

Fortunately, the dog was mine.
It may have been due to the dim lighting,
but the comfortable shape, the soft coat, and the
proud posture standing erect on all four legs
were identical to the chair beside her.

To my dear dog, Isotta

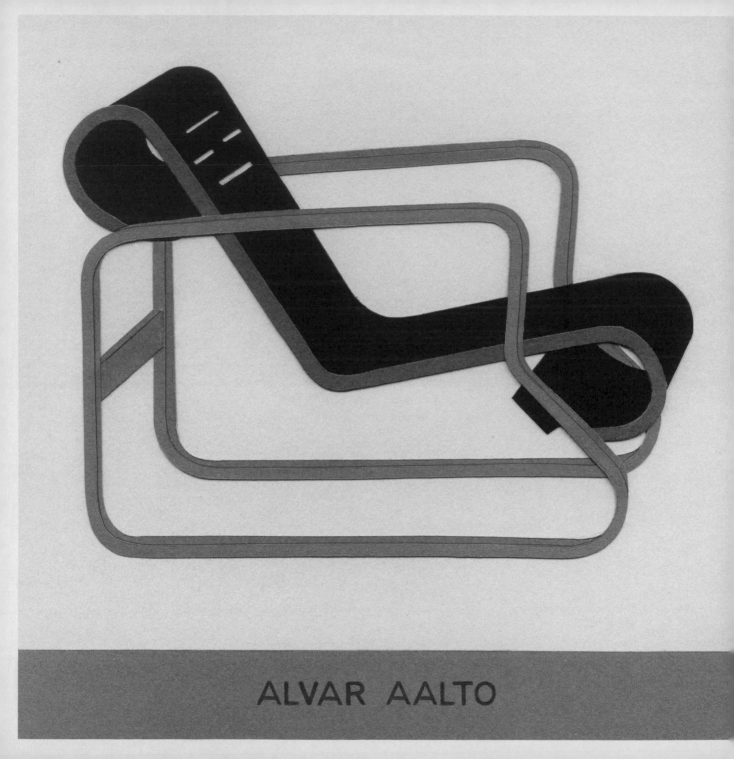

ALVAR AALTO

DOBERMANN

EERO AARNIO

BULLDOG

FRANCO ALBINI

MINIATURE POODLE

RON ARAD

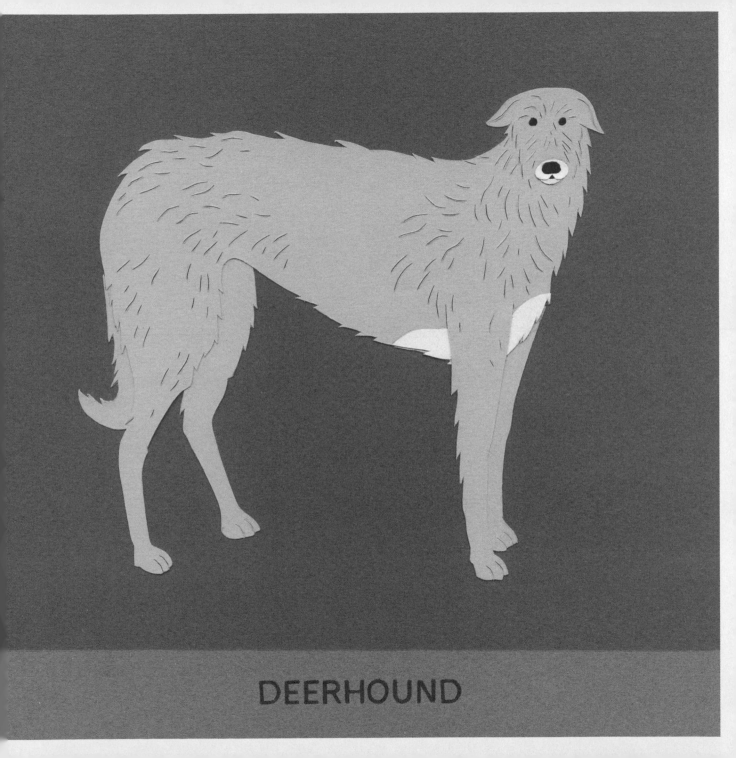

DEERHOUND

HARRY BERTOIA

BULL TERRIER

ANDREA BRANZI

ARIÉGEOIS

LUIGI CACCIA DOMINIONI

PUG

NORMAN CHERNER

ITALIAN POINTING DOG

MICHELE DE LUCCHI

DALMATIAN

TOM DIXON

STANDARD POODLE

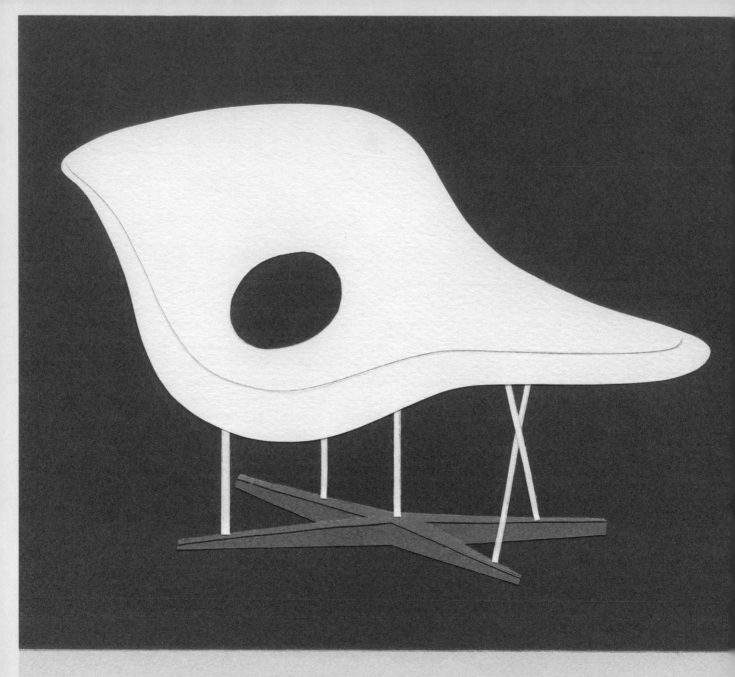

CHARLES AND RAY EAMES

BILLY

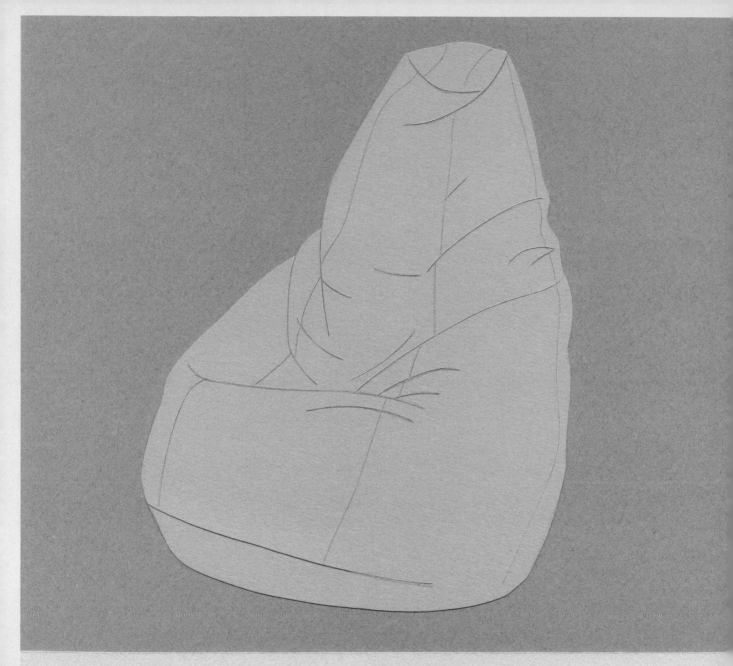

GATTI PAOLINO TEODORO

BOLOGNESE

FRANK GEHRY

SHAR PEI

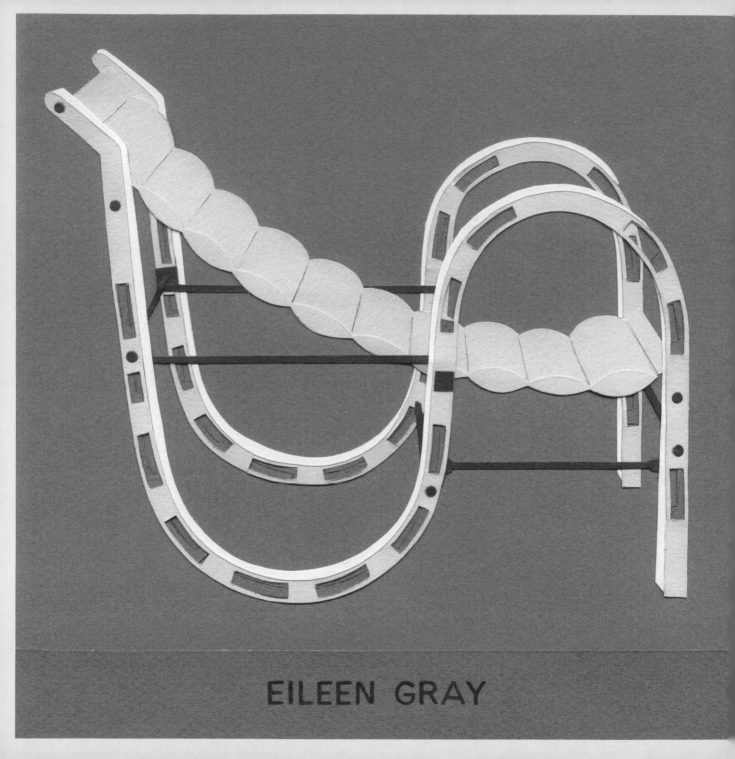

EILEEN GRAY

IBIZAN PODENCO

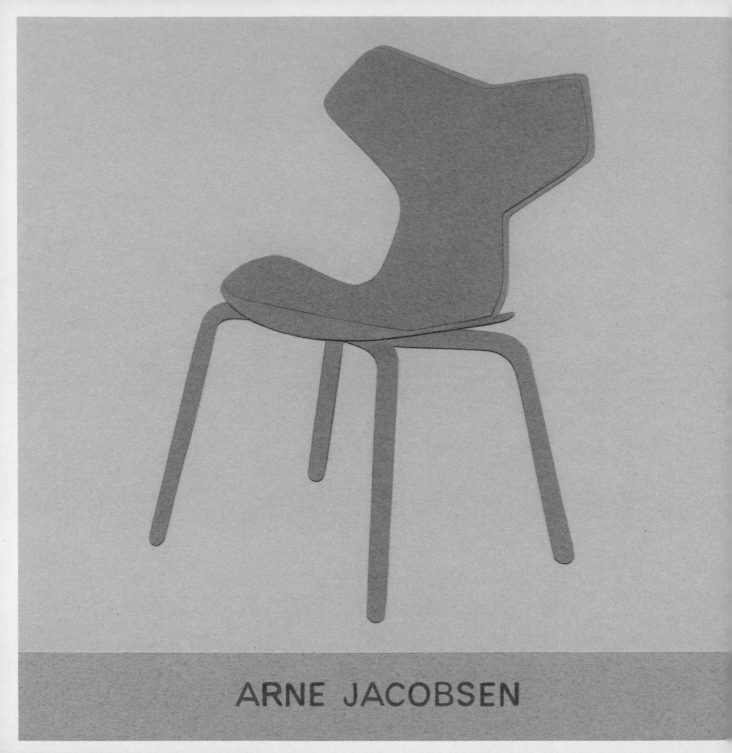

ARNE JACOBSEN

WELSH CORGI

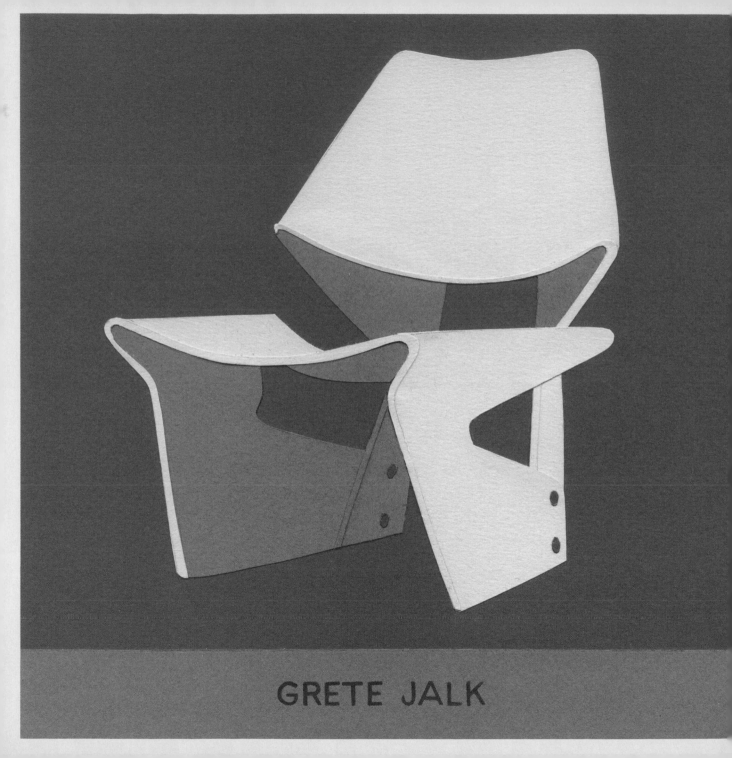

GRETE JALK

AKITA

IB KOFOD-LARSEN

SPANISH HOUND

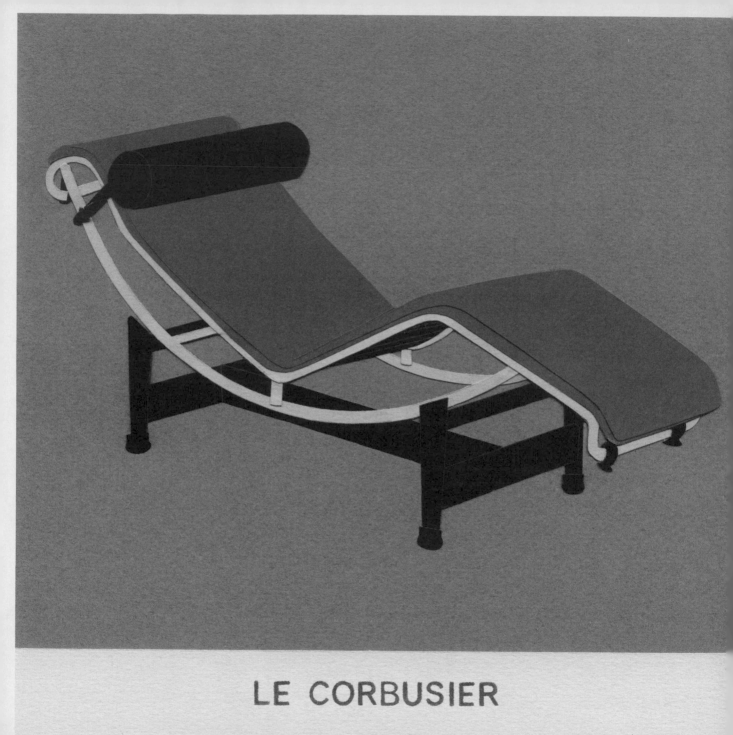

LE CORBUSIER

SPANISH GREYHOUND

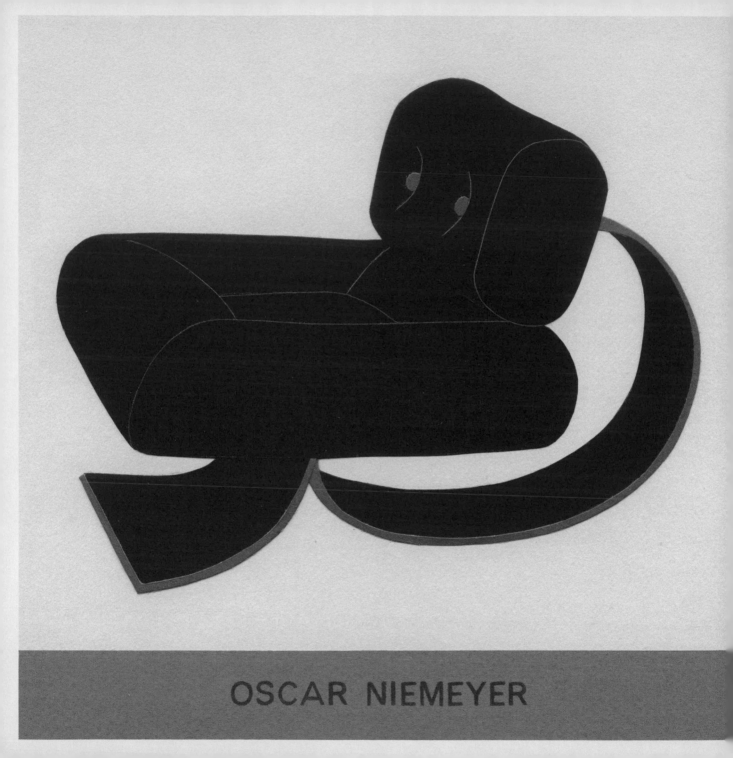

OSCAR NIEMEYER

AFFENPINSCHER

VERNER PANTON

MEDIUM-SIZED ANGLO-FRENCH HOUND

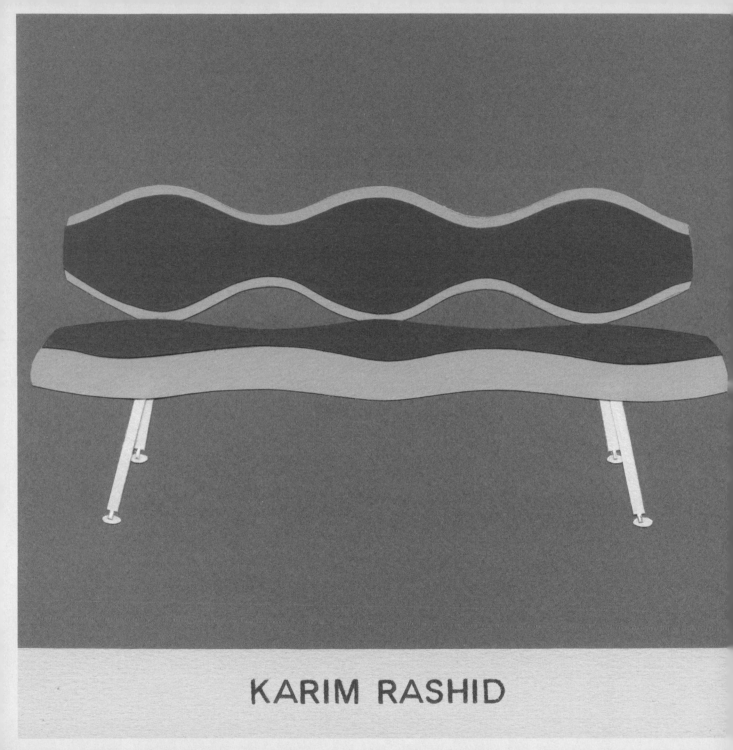

KARIM RASHID

ROMAGNA WATER DOG

EERO SAARINEN

ITALIAN VOLPINO

PHILIPPE STARCK

FOX TERRIER

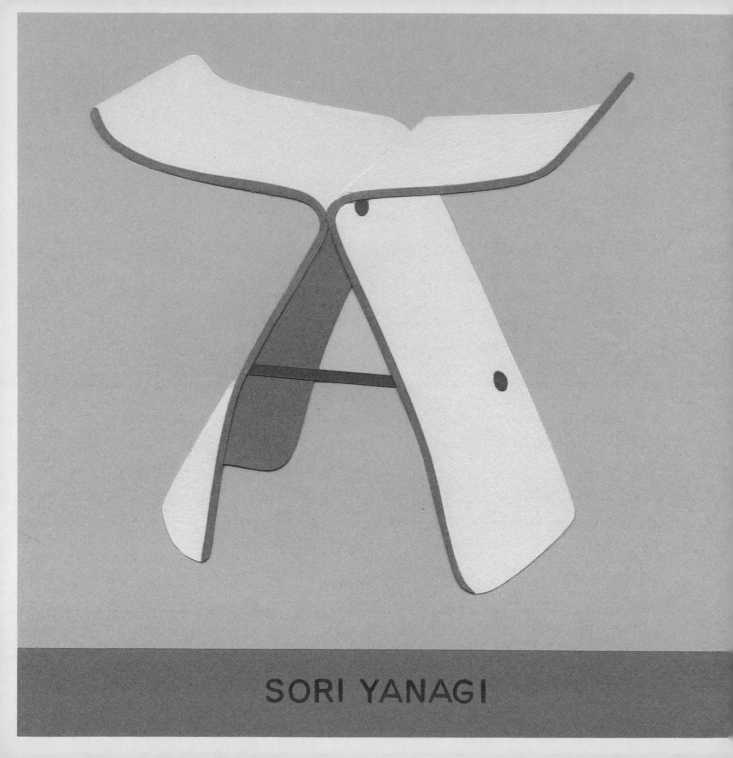

SORI YANAGI

AFGHAN HOUND

List of the
CHAIRS AND DOGS

Name: 41 Paimio
Designer: Alvar Aalto
Date: 1930–31
Producer: Huonekalu-ja
Rakennustyötehdas; reissued
by Artek from 1935 to present
Material: Bent plywood, bent
laminated birch frame

Name: Ball Chair
Designer: Eero Aarnio
Date: 1963
Producer: Asko 1966–80;
reissued by Adelta from 1992
to present
Material: Fibreglass,
upholstered in fabric

Name: Tre Pezzi
Designer: Franco Albini
Date: 1959
Producer: Cassina
Material: Tubular steel frame,
painted matt black or chrome-
plated; padded elements
upholstered in fabric or leather

Name: Victoria and Albert Sofa
Designer: Ron Arad
Date: 2000
Producer: Moroso
Material: Reinforced fibreglass
with steel support, upholstered
in stress-resistant polyurethane
foam; legs in painted steel with
adjustable chromed feet

Name: Diamond Chair
Designer: Harry Bertoia
Date: 1952
Producer: Knoll
Material: Bent and welded
steel rod construction with
chrome or vinyl finish; cover
in boucle, vinyl or ultrasuede

Name: Revers
Designer: Andrea Branzi
Date: 1993
Producer: Cassina
Material: Metallized grey
lacquered aluminum frame,
curved beech plywood seat;
a curved strip of solid beech
forms the back and armrests

Name: Catilina
Designer: Luigi Caccia Dominioni
Date: 1957
Producer: Azucena
Material: Iron or stainless
steel frame, black gloss-
lacquered seat, cushion in
expanded polyurethane covered
in leather, velvet or fabric

Name: Cherner
Designer: Norman Cherner
Date: 1957
Producer: Plycraft; reissued
by the Cherner Chair Company
from 1999 to present
Material: Moulded plywood
faced in walnut

Name: First
Designer: Michele De Lucchi
Date: 1983
Producer: Memphis
Material: Tubular steel frame with enamelled wood seat, back and armrests

Name: Wingback
Designer: Tom Dixon
Date: 2008
Producer: George Smith
Material: Solid birch frame stuffed with layers of natural cotton and boar bristle

Name: La Chaise
Designer: Charles & Ray Eames
Date: 1948
Producer: Vitra
Material: Fibreglass seat shell on an oak and steel rod base

Name: Sacco
Designer: Gatti, Paolini, Teodoro
Date: 1968
Producer: Zanotta
Material: Canvas, leather or synthetic envelope filled with highly resistant expanded polystyrene pellets

Name: Wiggle
Designer: Frank Gehry
Date: 1972
Producer: Jack Brogan 1972–73; reissued by Vitra from 1992 as Wiggle Side Chair
Material: Laminated corrugated cardboard construction

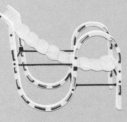

Name: S Chair
Designer: Eileen Gray
Date: 1938
Producer: Jean Désert
Material: Upholstered seat in a dramatically curved, adjustable metal frame; also known as the folding hammock chair

Name: Grand Prix
Designer: Arne Jacobsen
Date: 1957
Producer: Fritz Hansen
Material: Pressure-moulded veneer shell; legs in matching wood or chromed tubular steel

Name: GJ Chair
Designer: Grete Jalk
Date: 1963
Producer: Poul Jeppesen 1963–64; Lange Production 2008 to present
Material: Moulded plywood construction faced in black-stained ash, Oregon pine or teak, with steel bolts

Name: Shell
Designer: Ib Kofod-Larsen
Date: 1950s
Producer: Christensen & Larsen
Material: Back and seat in teak-veneered bent plywood, frame in solid beech

Name: Chaise Longue LC4
Designer: Le Corbusier
Date: 1928
Producer: Cassina
Material: Adjustable chrome-plated steel frame on a black enamelled steel base, upholstered in leather, hide or canvas; headrest padded with polyester

Name: Club Chair
Designer: Oscar Niemeyer
Date: 1978
Producer: Tendo Brasileira
Material: Leather upholstery on a lacquered wood frame with plastic fittings (early models made with stainless steel frames by Mobilier International, c. 1970)

Name: Panton
Designer: Verner Panton
Date: 1960
Producer: Vitra
Material: Durable, dyed-through plastic (previously foam or thermoplastic; polypropylene from 1999)

Name: Wavelength 3-seater
Designer: Karim Rashid
Date: 2000
Producer: Nienkämper
Material: Upholstered in leather, vinyl or fabric; cast aluminum base in a brushed or polished finish

Name: Tulip, Model no. 150
Designer: Eero Saarinen
Date: 1955–56
Producer: Knoll
Material: Fibreglass seat shell on a plastic-coated aluminium stem; loose foam cushion

Name: Costes
Designer: Philippe Starck
Date: 1984
Producer: Driade
Material: Painted tubular steel frame with bent mahogany-faced plywood back and leather-covered foam seat

Name: Butterfly
Designer: Sori Yanagi
Date: 1956
Producer: Tendo Mokko; now manufactured by Vitra
Material: Moulded plywood with brass stretcher and fittings

Breed: Dobermann
Classification: Pinscher and Schnauzer type
Origin: Germany
Size: M 68–72 cm (26 ¾–28 ¼ in.), F 63–68 cm (24 ¾–26 ¾ in.) (height at shoulder)
Temperament: Devoted to the family and loves children; self-confident, alert and intrepid

Breed: Bulldog
Classification: Molossoid breeds, Mastiff type
Origin: Great Britain
Size: 31–40 cm (12 ¼–15 ¾ in.)
Temperament: Gentle, dependable and courageous; fierce in appearance but an affectionate companion dog

Breed: Miniature Poodle
Classification: Poodle
Origin: France
Size: 28–35 cm (11–13 ¾ in.)
Temperament: Renowned for its loyalty, capable of learning and being trained; a particularly pleasant companion dog

Breed: Deerhound
Classification: Rough-haired Sighthounds
Origin: Great Britain
Size: M minimum 76 cm (30 in.), F minimum 71 cm (28 in.)
Temperament: Docile and friendly, obedient and eager to please; never aggressive or nervous

Breed: Bull Terrier
Classification: Bull-type Terriers
Origin: Great Britain
Size: 51–61 cm (20–24 in.)
Temperament: Courageous and spirited, with a fun-loving attitude. Obstinate and requires firm training, but particularly good with people

Breed: Ariégeois
Classification: Medium-sized Hounds
Origin: France
Size: M 52–58 cm (20 ½–22 ¾ in.), F 50–56 cm (19 ¾–22 in.)
Temperament: Happy and sociable, easy to train, with a resounding voice

Breed: Pug
Classification: Small Molossian type
Origin: China
Size: M 30–36 cm (11 ¾–14 in.), F 25–30 cm (9 ¾–11 ¾ in.)
Temperament: Great charm, dignity and intelligence; even-tempered and happy, with a lively disposition

Breed: Italian Pointing Dog
Classification: Continental Pointing Dogs, 'Braque' type
Origin: Italy
Size: M 58–67 cm (22 ¾–26 ½ in.), F 55–62 cm (21 ¾–24 ½ in.)
Temperament: Reliable, endowed with an excellent ability to understand, docile

Breed: Dalmatian
Classification: Scenthounds and related breeds
Origin: Croatia
Size: M 56–62 cm (22–24 ½ in.), F 54–60 cm (21 ¼–23 ½ in.)
Temperament: Friendly, not nervous or aggressive; loves water and outdoor activities

Breed: Standard Poodle
Classification: Poodle
Origin: France
Size: 45–60 cm (17 ¾–23 ½ in.)
Temperament: Highly intelligent, energetic and sociable, with a kindly demeanour and love of playing games

Breed: Billy
Classification: Large-sized Hounds
Origin: France
Size: M 60–70 cm (23 ½–27 ½ in.), F 58–62 cm (22 ¾–24 ½ in.)
Temperament: Intelligent and courageous; like most large hounds difficult off the lead and extremely fast

Breed: Bolognese
Classification: Bichons and related breeds
Origin: Italy
Size: M 27–30 cm (10 ¾–11 ¾ in.), F 25–28 cm (9 ¾–11 in.)
Temperament: Serious, not very active, enterprising, docile, very much attached to its master and his entourage

Breed: Shar Pei
Classification: Molossian, Mastiff type
Origin: China
Size: 44–51 cm (17 ¼–20 in.)
Temperament: Calm, independent and loyal; affectionate to its family

Breed: Ibizan Podenco
Classification: Primitive-type Hunting Dogs
Origin: Spain (Balearic Islands)
Size: M 66–72 cm (26–28 ¼ in.), F 60–67 cm (23 ½–26 ½ in.)
Temperament: Intelligent, active, stubborn, independent and sensitive

Breed: Welsh Corgi
Classification: Sheepdogs
Origin: Great Britain
Size: 25–30 cm (9 ¾–11 ¾ in.)
Temperament: Bold in outlook and workmanlike; affectionate, outgoing and friendly; never nervous or aggressive

Breed: Akita
Classification: Asian Spitz and related breeds
Origin: Japan
Size: M 66–71 cm (26–28 in.), F 61–66 cm (24–26 in.)
Temperament: Composed, faithful, docile and receptive

Breed: Spanish Hound
Classification: Medium-sized Hounds
Origin: Spain
Size: M 52–57 cm (20 ½–22 ½ in.), F 48–53 cm (19–20 ¾ in.)
Temperament: Affectionate and calm; shows extraordinary courage and bravery when hunting game

Breed: Spanish Greyhound
Classification: Short-haired Sighthounds
Origin: Spain
Size: M 62–70 cm (24 ½–27 ½ in.), F 60–68 cm (23 ½–26 ¾ in.)
Temperament: Serious temperament; reserved on occasion, but an energetic and lively hunter

Breed: Affenpinscher
Classification: Pinscher and Schnauzer type
Origin: Germany
Size: 25–30 cm (9 ¾–11 ¾ in.)
Temperament: Fearless, alert, persistent and devoted; sometimes quick-tempered and passionate; an agreeable family dog

Breed: Medium-sized Anglo-French Hound
Classification: Medium-sized Hounds
Origin: France
Size: 48–56 cm (19–22 in.)
Temperament: Strong, combative, energetic and affectionate to its owner

Breed: Romagna Water Dog
Classification: Water Dogs
Origin: Italy
Size: M 43–48 cm (17–19 in.), F 41–46 cm (16 ¼–18 in.)
Temperament: Tractable and undemanding, keenly affectionate and very attached to its owner

Breed: Italian Volpino
Classification: European Spitz
Origin: Italy
Size: M 27–30 cm (10 ¾–11 ¾ in.), F 25–28 cm (9 ¾–11 in.)
Temperament: Very attached to its environment and family; has a very distinctive temperament, lively and playful

Breed: Fox Terrier
Classification: Large and Medium-sized Terriers
Origin: Great Britain
Size: 26–39 cm (10 ¼–15 ¼ in.)
Temperament: Alert, quick of movement, keen of expression, friendly and fearless

Breed: Afghan Hound
Classification: Long-haired or fringed sighthounds
Origin: Great Britain
Size: M 68–74 cm (26 ¾–29 in.), F 63–69 cm (24 ¾–27 ¼ in.)
Temperament: Dignified and aloof, high-spirited and sensitive, with a high prey drive and low obedience

Cristina Amodeo is a freelance illustrator
and graphic designer based in Milan. She
created the illustrations in this book using
cut-paper collage. Her two previous books,
Matisse's Garden, with Samantha Friedman,
and *Toujours avec moi*, with Laura Brugnoli,
have delighted children across Europe
and America.

First published in the United Kingdom in 2015
by Thames & Hudson Ltd
181A High Holborn, London WC1V 7QX

Dogs and Chairs © 2015 Cristina Amodeo

Project Editor: Debbie Bibo

British Library Cataloguing-in-Publication Data
A catalogue record for this book is available from
the British Library

ISBN 978-0-500-51816-8

Printed and bound in China by Toppan Leefung
Printing Limited

To find out about all our publications,
please visit **www.thamesandhudson.com**.
There you can subscribe to our e-newsletter,
browse or download our current catalogue,
and buy any titles that are in print.